TEEN LIFE™

FREQUENTLY ASKED QUESTIONS ABOUT

Everyday First Aid

Heather Hasan

ROSEN
PUBLISHING®

New York

To my niece, Molly: I hope you
don't get too many boo-boos

Published in 2010 by The Rosen Publishing Group, Inc.
29 East 21st Street, New York, NY 10010

Library of Congress Cataloging-in-Publication Data

Hasan, Heather.
Frequently asked questions about everyday first aid /
Heather Hasan.—1st ed.
      p. cm.—(FAQ: teen life)
Includes bibliographical references and index.
ISBN-13: 978-1-4358-5326-3 (library binding)
1. First aid in illness and injury—Popular works. I. Title.
RC87.H337 2010
616.02'52—dc22

                                              2008054404

Manufactured in the United States of America

Contents

Chapter one

HOW DO I TREAT SCRAPES, CUTS, SPLINTERS, BLISTERS, AND BURNS?

A scrape, or abrasion, is caused when the skin is rubbed off. Scrapes usually result from the skin being dragged across a hard surface. It is the injury that occurs when you fall off your skateboard and slide down the driveway. With a scrape or abrasion, the outer layer of skin is damaged, so there will be some bleeding and oozing.

Cuts to the skin are caused by sharp things like knives, broken glass, or razors. Sometimes the edges of cuts are smooth. Such smooth cuts are called incisions. Other times, the skin is torn and the wound is jagged. This type of injury is called a laceration. Both incisions and lacerations tend to bleed heavily due to the breaking of many superficial blood vessels in the skin.

When treating minor lacerations and abrasions, the first thing you want to do is wash your hands with a lot of

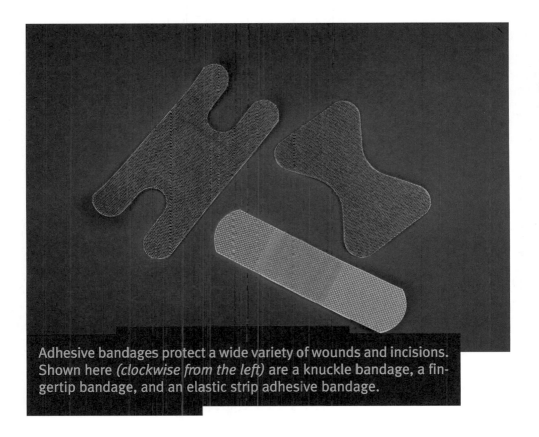

Adhesive bandages protect a wide variety of wounds and incisions. Shown here *(clockwise from the left)* are a knuckle bandage, a fingertip bandage, and an elastic strip adhesive bandage.

soap and water. Then briskly wash the wound to remove any debris. Hold the wound under running water and gently clean away any dirt with soap. With a scrape, you may need to use tweezers to pluck out debris. Remember to wash the ends of the tweezers with alcohol first.

After cleaning the area, attempt to stop any bleeding. (Vigorous washing after a clot has formed will just wash out the clot and cause the wound to bleed again.) Apply strong pressure to stop the bleeding. Press some sterile gauze or a cloth firmly against the wound. Elevating the wound may help stop the bleeding, too.

Once the bleeding has stopped, clean the wound with an antiseptic wash to prevent infection. Then apply some antibiotic ointment and cover the wound with a bandage or piece of gauze, secured with first-aid tape. If a cut is a little deeper and the edges are not next to one another, you may need to put a butterfly bandage on it. This type of bandage is designed to pull the skin together and reduce the chance of scarring and infection.

See a doctor if a scrape or cut is very large or if the edges are very far apart. You may need to get stitches. You should also see a doctor if the wound is too painful for you to clean yourself. Dirt and other debris can enter any break in the skin and cause infection. If you have any signs of infection—for instance, increased pain, swelling, or redness; pus in the wound; or a fever—then you should seek medical attention. If a wound is very dirty or was caused by rusty metal, you may have to worry about tetanus. Tetanus is a potentially fatal disease that is caused by bacteria, which can be found in dirt. This disease affects the muscles of the neck and jaw. An early symptom of tetanus is the stiffening of the jaw muscles. If you have not had a tetanus shot in the last five years, you may need to get one. Ask your doctor.

To avoid scrapes and lacerations, use care. When biking or skateboarding, wear protective gear like a helmet and kneepads. Wearing long pants and a long-sleeved shirt also helps protect your skin when you're playing hard. Use caution when using a knife or other sharp objects, or ask someone to help. Never pick up or throw anything sharp that you find on the ground.

Splinters

A splinter is a small piece of wood, metal, stone, glass, or other material that has broken off of a larger piece. A splinter may be partly sticking out of the skin, or it may be buried within the skin. A splinter in the skin causes mild pain, redness, and swelling.

Before removing a splinter, wash your hands with soap and water. If the splinter is sticking out of the skin, clean some tweezers with alcohol and use them to grasp the exposed

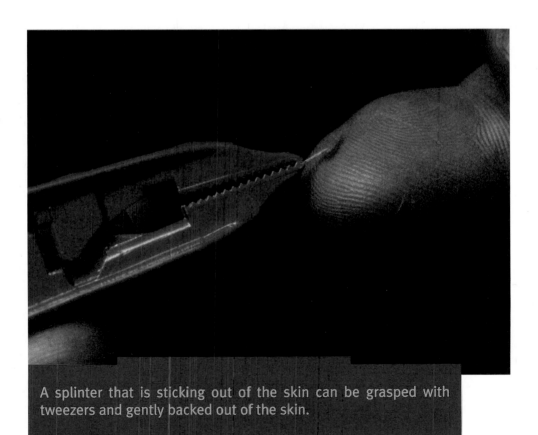

A splinter that is sticking out of the skin can be grasped with tweezers and gently backed out of the skin.

piece. Pull the splinter out of the skin in the same direction that it went in.

If a splinter is below the skin, soak that part of your body in warm water for about ten minutes. This can encourage the splinter to come to the surface. After soaking it, gently rub each side of the splinter with a washcloth. This will rub some of the skin away from the splinter and may bring it to the surface.

If you're still having trouble reaching the splinter, clean a needle with alcohol and use it to scrape away the surrounding skin until the splinter is exposed. Then use the tweezers to pull it out. Once the splinter is out, put some antibiotic ointment on it and cover it with a bandage.

If a splinter is very large or very deep, you should visit a doctor. A doctor can remove your large splinter under sterile conditions. You should also see a doctor if you show any signs of infection. These include increased pain, redness, swelling, pus, or fever.

To prevent getting a splinter, wear shoes when playing on a wooden surface or walking around outside. Wear gloves when working with wood. You should also avoid sliding your hands across rough wooden surfaces.

Blisters

A blister is a fluid-filled sac that has just a thin layer of skin covering it. Blisters form on the skin when the skin is irritated by something rubbing against it. Most blisters form on the feet when shoes rub against the skin. Hands are also susceptible to

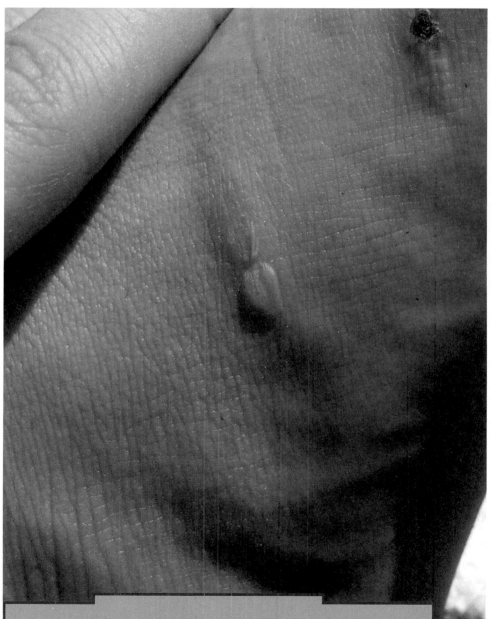

To prevent blisters, like this one, from forming, cover the irritated area with moleskin, a bandage, or even duct tape. This will prevent further friction to the skin.

blisters when doing activities such as yard work or playing sports. The first sign that a blister is forming is a "hot spot" on the skin. The skin can be red and painful, too.

If a blister is smaller than a quarter, you can protect it from further rubbing with a flexible bandage strip or a small "doughnut" bandage. You can make your own doughnut-shaped bandage out of foam. Make sure the hole in the center is larger than your blister so that no part of the foam comes into contact with the blister. This way, the foam will take all of the pressure and rubbing instead of your skin. Place the doughnut bandage over the blister with the blister in the center. Secure it with first-aid tape.

If the blister is the size of a quarter or larger, it may be better to pop it under very clean conditions instead of waiting for it to pop on its own in dirty conditions. First, wash your hands well with warm water and soap. Then wash the blister. Clean a needle with alcohol, and use the needle to make a tiny pinprick in the skin covering the fluid. It will not hurt because the skin over the blister is already dead. Once the fluid has drained from the blister, apply an antibiotic ointment and cover it with a bandage or a gauze pad that is secured with first-aid tape.

Burns

Burns are injuries to the skin that can be caused by flames, hot objects, electrical currents, chemicals, or radiation (a kind of energy wave). Burns are classified by the depth or degree of

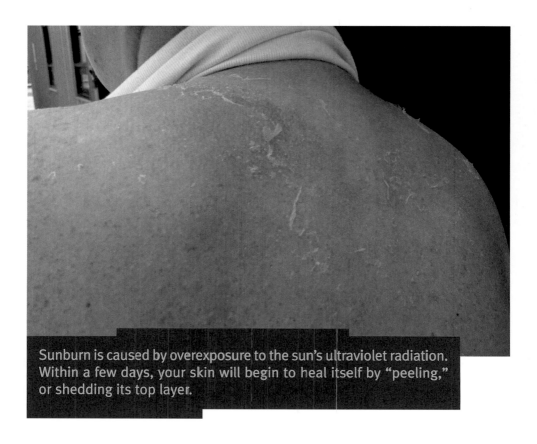

Sunburn is caused by overexposure to the sun's ultraviolet radiation. Within a few days, your skin will begin to heal itself by "peeling," or shedding its top layer.

skin damage. There are first-degree burns, second-degree burns, and third-degree burns.

First-degree burns, also called superficial burns, are mild and involve only the outside layer of the skin. They are usually caused by overexposure to the sun (sunburn), scalding by hot water or steam, or brief contact with a hot object. With a first-degree burn, the skin is reddened. Someone with a first-degree burn usually experiences mild swelling and pain.

Second-degree, or partial-thickness, burns cause injury to the layers of skin beneath the surface skin. Second-degree burns result from scalding with boiling water, deep sunburn, and flash burns from substances like gasoline and kerosene. Second-degree burns are characterized by blistering of the skin. A blister is a painful swelling of the skin that contains fluid. With second-degree burns, redness and swelling for several days following the injury are common. The skin may also appear moist and oozy with a second-degree burn.

Third-degree, or full-thickness, burns involve all three layers of skin. Third-degree burns result in the loss of skin, hair follicles, and sweat glands. For these reasons, third-degree burns require surgical skin grafts. Skin grafting is basically removing damaged skin and replacing it with healthy skin taken from another part of the body.

With any burn, it is important to first remove yourself from the source of the burn. With first- and second-degree burns, you should immediately put the burned area under cold running water or submerge it in cold water. You could also apply a cold-water compress. A clean towel, a washcloth, or a handkerchief can be used as a compress. Cold water helps to cool down the skin and relieve pain. Ice should not be applied to a burn because ice can cause further damage to the skin. Neither should grease or butter be applied to burns. After the burn has been cooled, aloe vera gel may be applied only if there are no blisters present. Blisters that have formed on the skin should not be broken. Otherwise, bacteria could get in the wound and cause infection. Allow the burn to dry, then cover it loosely with a clean, dry bandage.

First-degree burns and mild second-degree burns usually do not require medical attention. Immediate medical attention is definitely needed, though, if a large area of the body is burned or if there is lots of blistering or skin damage. Also, breathing problems could develop if a person has flash burns around the nose or lips. In this case, the injured person should be seen promptly in an emergency room. Third-degree burns definitely require immediate medical help. Third-degree burns turn the skin white and hard and cause little pain.

There are many ways to prevent burns. Do not ever play with fire. Keep hot liquids away from the edge of a table or counter, and keep pot and pan handles turned away from the edge of the stove. Be especially careful with small children around hot stoves or with boiling liquids. Before you eat, check to see how hot the food is. Cover up or apply sunscreen before you spend time in the sun.

WHAT SHOULD I DO IF I AM BITTEN OR STUNG?

A bite from any animal—whether it's a wild animal or just a pet—could result in an open wound. The most common pet bites are dog bites. Dog bites can cause more physical damage to the tissue than cat bites. However, cat bites can be more dangerous. Cats have a wider variety of bacteria in their mouths. A cat bite can cause cat scratch fever, a bacterial disease that causes fever, headache, fatigue, and a poor appetite. It should be treated with antibiotics.

If you are bitten by an animal (or a human), treat it like you would treat a scrape or an abrasion. First, irrigate the site with lots of warm, soapy water. Then stop any bleeding with gauze or cloth. Press firmly with the palm of your hand and raise the wound above the level of your heart. Once the bleeding has stopped, wash the wound well with warm, soapy water.

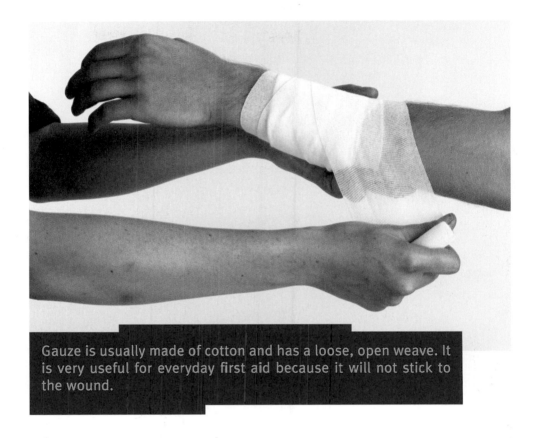

Gauze is usually made of cotton and has a loose, open weave. It is very useful for everyday first aid because it will not stick to the wound.

If a bandage is too small to cover the wound, cover it with a piece of gauze and secure it with first-aid tape. Apply ice to alleviate any swelling. You should call your doctor about any bite that breaks the skin. Animal bites (as well as human bites) can cause tetanus. The best way to avoid being bitten by pets is to be gentle with them. Always ask the owner if you can pet them before doing so.

If you are bitten by a wild animal, you may have to worry about rabies. Rabies is a contagious infection of the central nervous system that is caused by a virus. The central nervous

A first-aid kit is essential when hiking. The kit should contain medical supplies for bites, burns, and scratches, as well as safety items for warmth, shelter, health, navigation, and nourishment.

system includes the brain and the spinal cord. The virus enters the body when an infected animal bites a person. The animals that are most likely to be infected with rabies are foxes, skunks, bats, coyotes, and raccoons. If you think you've been bitten by a rabid animal, you must seek immediate medical attention. In the meantime, wash the wound with soap and water and apply a dressing. It is best not to touch wild animals at all.

A human bite that breaks the skin could cause infection. The human mouth is full of bacteria. (The average human mouth contains about six hundred different types of bacteria.) Animal bites can become infected, too. If you experience increased pain, swelling, or redness around the wound within the day following the bite, this indicates an infection. Other signs of infection include fever, streaking, or pus draining from the wound. If you have any of these symptoms, you should see a doctor.

Snake Bites

There are two general types of poisonous snakes: coral snakes and pit vipers. Pit vipers include rattlesnakes, water moccasins (or cottonmouths), and copperheads. Pit vipers are the most common source of poisonous snake bites in the United States and Canada. One way to quickly tell the difference between a poisonous snake and a nonpoisonous snake is the shape of the head. Viewed from above, a poisonous snake has a triangular head, while a non-poisonous snake has a more tapered head.

If a poisonous snake bites you, you could get really sick or even die. Seek immediate medical help. Until help arrives, remain still and keep the bite below heart level. Do not apply ice to the bite. With a venomous snake bite, this can cause further skin damage.

If you are absolutely sure the snake that bit you is not venomous, wash the wound thoroughly with soap and water. Apply an antibiotic and a bandage. Ask your doctor if you need a tetanus shot. Even with a nonpoisonous snake bite, you should seek medical attention.

The best way to avoid a snake bite is not to touch snakes! Stand still if you see a snake. The snake will most likely just slither away. When outdoors, keep your hands out of holes, stumps, and hollow logs. These are great places for snakes to curl up. When walking or hiking in an area where snakes are abundant, it may be a good idea to wear boots and long pants. When going through a woodpile, you may want to wear gloves.

Bee Stings

Some of the most common stinging insects are bees, wasps, yellow jackets, hornets, and bumblebees. These insects may be little, but their stings can be hugely painful. Besides the pain, stings from these insects can cause redness, swelling, and warmth. The sting site is usually warm, red, and puffy, with a white spot in the center. The area may also itch. These symptoms are a result of the body's reaction to the insect's venom. If the insect has left behind its stinger, you will want to remove it very carefully. Otherwise, it will continue to allow venom to

Because of its barbs, the stinger of a honeybee will be torn from its body when it stings a mammal or bird. The victim's skin may continue to absorb venom from a detached stinger.

absorb into the skin. First, wash your hands with soap and water. Then use a magnifying glass to locate the stinger. It should look like a small sliver. The stinger needs to be scraped out as a whole piece. Pulling it out or breaking it off would result in more venom being squeezed out. Once you're sure the stinger is gone, wash the area with soap and water. Then apply an ice pack to the area. This will decrease the amount of venom that your body absorbs. It will also decrease the spread of the venom. To relieve itching and discomfort, use soothing lotions like calamine. To prevent a sting from these insects, try not to look or smell like a flower. Bright colors and sweet-smelling lotions and perfumes are attractive to insects like bees. Also, make sure you cover up your sweet-smelling drinks. Bees may crawl inside to investigate, and they could sting your lips or mouth when you take a sip.

Some people can have a severe allergic reaction to insect bites, especially bee stings. Symptoms of a life-threatening allergic reaction include weakness, coughing or wheezing, difficulty breathing, nausea or vomiting, dizziness, severe itching, and severe swelling in parts of the body other than the sting site. A person experiencing such symptoms should seek immediate medical attention by calling 911.

Stings from Scorpions, Fire Ants, and Spiders

Scorpions, fire ants, and some spiders inject venom when they sting or bite. Scorpions live in warm, dry regions that include the southwestern United States. They inject venom from a stinger in their tails. Some types of scorpions are more poisonous than others. The stings from the really dangerous types of scorpions are usually intensely painful and hurt immediately. Some dangerous scorpions live in the deserts of Arizona, New Mexico, and California. The stings from these scorpions are rare but can be serious. If you think you may have been stung by a dangerous scorpion, seek medical attention right away. Stings from the less dangerous ones feel somewhat like a bee's sting. To relieve itching and pain, apply ice to the sting site. An over-the-counter antihistamine, such as Benadryl, can be taken as well. An antihistamine is a drug that treats allergies. If a person stung by any scorpion has a history of allergic reactions to insect bites or shows any signs of illness, get help at once.

The sting from a fire ant can be extremely painful. Most fire ants live in the southern United States and South America. Fire ants live in loose mounds of dirt and will swarm if they are disturbed. If you are bitten by fire ants, try not to break the tiny blisters that form. Wash the injured area well with soap and water. Cover it with a sterile bandage to prevent infection. Putting a paste made from baking soda and water on the sting may help soothe the pain.

In the United States, almost all spiders are relatively harmless to humans. However, the black widow spider and brown recluse spider are two exceptions. Black widow spiders are found in the southern United States and Canada. A black widow spider is shiny and black and has a red hourglass marking on its belly. A bite from a black widow spider causes only minor redness, swelling, and pain at the bite site. However, the bite can be dangerous, especially to children. Other symptoms of a black widow spider bite include stomach and back muscle cramps, nausea, heavy sweating, headache, numb and tingling palms and bottoms of feet, tightness in the chest, and difficulty breathing. Brown recluse spiders are also particularly harmful to children. They can be recognized by a dark brown, violin-shaped marking on the top front portion of their bodies. The bite of a brown recluse spider may turn red, white, and blue and sometimes develops

Bites from brown recluse spiders are rare. The spider is not aggressive and will usually bite only if pressed up against the skin, as when it is tangled up in clothes.

into a purplish blister. The pain from the bite usually worsens over time, and some people get fever, chills, nausea, joint pain, and a body rash. If you're bitten by either of these spiders, keep the bitten area lower than the heart, wrap the area in ice, and seek medical attention immediately.

Tick Bites

Tick bites are common. Ticks make their homes in woods and fields. They feed on the blood of animals and people. Once a tick gets on your skin, it travels to the warm, moist areas of your body, such as your armpits, groin, or scalp. A tick burrows its head into the skin and uses its fangs to suck the blood. Tick bites can cause itching, redness, and mild, hard swelling. Several diseases are transmitted by ticks. A red, circular rash that resembles a bull's eye could signal Lyme disease from a deer tick. If unnoticed, this tick's bite can result in a systemic illness within a few weeks. Another disease, Rocky Mountain spotted fever, is characterized by headache, fever, and the appearance of a patchy, rose-colored rash on the wrists and ankles. If you experience any of these symptoms, see a doctor. Before removing a tick, wash your hands with soap and water. Clean tweezers with alcohol and use them to grasp the tick close to its mouth parts. Pull straight out with a slow and steady motion. To reduce further exposure to tick fluids, do not twist, squeeze, or crush the tick. Be careful to make sure that you don't leave any tick parts in the skin. Once you are sure that all of the tick has been removed, clean the skin well with soap and warm water. Apply a small amount of antibiotic ointment.

Other Insect Bites

Other common insect bites include mosquito bites, gnat bites, chigger bites, and flea bites. Bites from these insects are irritating but not dangerous. To soothe such minor bites and stings, apply ice and anti-itch lotions like calamine to the area.

To prevent insect and arthropod stings, wear light-colored clothes. Insects tend to be attracted to bright or dark clothes. Light-colored clothes also make it easier to spot insects and arthropods, such as ticks. If you're going to spend time outside, don't use a lot of perfume or sweet-smelling lotions. It's also wise to use insect repellent. Treating your pets with flea-and-tick products can help keep you from getting bitten by such creatures, too.

Chapter three

WHAT SHOULD I DO FOR MUSCLE, BONE, OR JOINT INJURIES?

A joint is the place in the body where bones meet. Joints help make it possible for our bodies to move. Some examples of joints are the knee, elbow, ankle, and shoulder. During an accident, it is possible for a bone to become dislodged from its usual fitting in a joint. This type of injury is called a dislocation. Dislocation is usually caused by trauma, such as a fall or blow. A dislocated bone makes the joint look temporarily deformed and misshapen. It is also tender and painful when moved. You should never attempt to put a dislocated bone back into place. Doing so could damage the surrounding muscles, ligaments, nerves, and blood vessels. To keep the joint from moving, splint or sling the joint in the position that you found it. (See "Wrapping, Splinting, and Slinging an Injury" at the end of this chapter.) A dislocation requires immediate medical attention. In the meantime, you can ice the injured joint. Icing will cut down on the swelling by minimizing internal bleeding and reducing the buildup of fluid in and around the joint.

Muscle Cramps

Muscle cramps are painful. They can occur during exercise or even in the middle of the night. These cramps tend to happen in the foot, the thigh, and the calf of the leg. They're caused by the buildup of large amounts of lactic acid in the muscles. Lactic acid is produced by the muscles as the body breaks down sugar for energy. Massaging the cramping muscle stimulates circulation, helping the muscle to relax. You can also relieve a cramp in the foot by turning the toes upward and bending the foot back. Heating a cramped muscle can help. Sore muscles also can be relieved by alternating hot and cold showers. Start off with hot water for about two minutes, and then switch to cold water. Focus the spray on the sore areas. The change in temperature may help get the blood in the area flowing, forcing the lactic acid from the muscle. Stretching for at least fifteen minutes before and after exercising can help prevent muscle cramps.

To reduce instances of recurrent cramping, try increasing the amount of vitamin D in your diet. Foods like fish and milk are good sources of the vitamin. Your body also produces vitamin D from sunlight. You can try eating more calcium-rich foods, such as milk and leafy greens. Adding foods to your diet that are high in vitamin E, such as wheat germ, soybeans, and parsley, can

Stretching before strenuous activity can help prevent pain and injury. Stretching can also increase the blood flow to sore muscles to relieve tightness.

also help. If you often get leg cramps at night, this could be a sign of poor blood circulation. You should see a doctor. Muscle cramps may also be a sign of potassium insufficiency. Eat bananas or take a multivitamin.

Strains and Sprains

Excessive stretching, heavy lifting, overexertion, wrenching actions, twisting, or sudden movements can cause muscle fibers to overstretch or tear. This kind of injury is called a muscle strain or a pulled muscle. A strain may cause immediate pain. It could also take several hours for pain to begin. Other symptoms of muscle strain include tenderness, swelling, bruising, and restricted movement. These symptoms are caused by bleeding inside the muscle.

The fibers of ligaments can become overstretched or torn, too, by wrenching, twisting, or lifting movements. A ligament is tissue that connects bones to one another. Ligaments support the joints. When a ligament is simply overstretched, the injury is called a strain. Sometimes, the fibers of a ligament are overstretched and partially torn. This type of injury is called a sprain. Ligament injury causes tenderness, swelling, and pain that is made worse with movement. The joint may be unstable.

The best way to treat sprains and strains is with rest, ice, compression, and elevation of the injured parts. This technique is known as R.I.C.E. (See "The R.I.C.E. Technique" on next page.) Avoid doing activities that cause increased pain. Consult a doctor to determine the extent of the injury. A doctor can decide

Of all joint sprains, ankle and knee sprains are the most common. Note the discoloration and swelling around this sprained ankle.

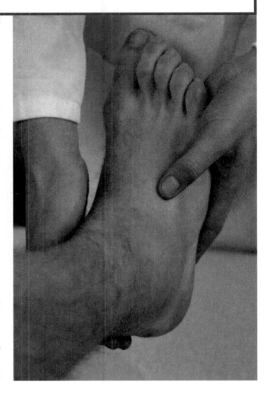

if crutches or a brace is needed, how restricted your activity should be, and if rehabilitation exercises are necessary for healing.

The R.I.C.E. Technique

Rest the body part to reduce bleeding in the injured muscle. Rest also reduces the risk for further damage and allows time for the tissue to heal.

Ice helps reduce the pain and swelling. Apply ice for ten minutes every few hours for the first two days following an injury. Crushed ice works best because it is able to evenly distribute the coldness. If you don't have crushed ice, a bag of frozen peas will work just as well. Just remember never to apply ice directly to the skin.

Compress the injured area to limit bleeding and swelling. Compression also helps give support to the injured area. Wrap

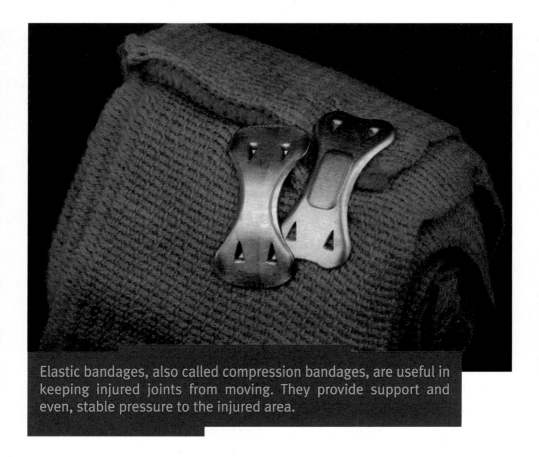

Elastic bandages, also called compression bandages, are useful in keeping injured joints from moving. They provide support and even, stable pressure to the injured area.

an elastic bandage firmly, but not too tightly, around the injured area. (See "Wrapping, Splinting, and Slinging an Injury" at the end of this chapter.) A compression bandage should be worn on the injured area for at least two days. Loosen the bandage if it is restricting the flow of blood.

Elevate the injured muscle to reduce swelling and bleeding. If possible, the injured part should be elevated higher than the heart. This helps drain excess fluid from the injured tissue.

If there is no swelling after two days, you can speed up the healing by applying heat to the injured area. This will get blood flowing around the injury. You can do this with a heating pad, a warm bottle, or a warm soak in the tub. Seek medical help if the pain or swelling is severe or if you suspect a bone may be broken.

Fractures

A fracture is a cracked or broken bone. If a person's bones are healthy, it usually takes a strong force to cause a serious fracture. Serious fractures can happen more easily in young children because their bones are softer. In some cases, a person may feel or hear a popping sound as the bone breaks. A fracture causes severe pain at the time of injury. Following the injury, it will hurt when the skin over the fracture is pressed upon. The site of a fracture may be swollen and have a bluish coloration. This is caused by internal bleeding at the site. The injured part may have limited or no mobility as well. The victim may feel a grating sensation as the ends of the fractured bones rub together. The injured part may appear deformed.

Fractures require medical care. In the meantime, there are some things that you can do. Keep the injured part immobile, or still. You can do this by splinting or slinging the injured part in the position that it was found (See "Wrapping, Splinting, and Slinging an Injury" below.) Just like with strains and sprains, you can use the R.I.C.E. technique for broken bones. (See "The R.I.C.E. Technique" above.) In fact, R.I.C.E. can be used for

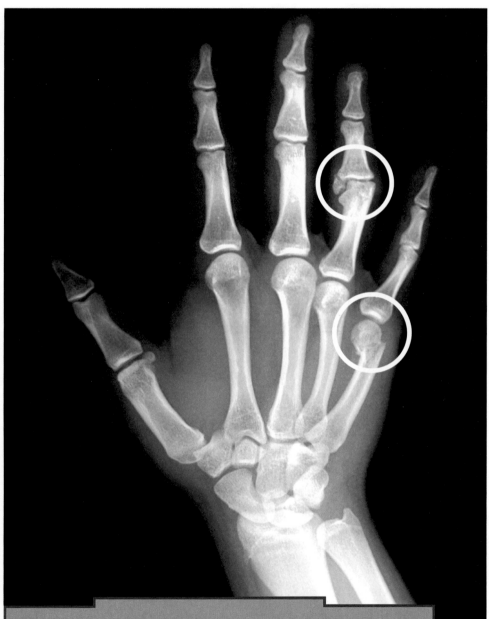

If a broken bone is suspected, a doctor will order an X-ray. The white circles on this X-ray show the location of fractures in a patient's finger and hand bones.

serious injuries as well as for minor ones, such as sore fingers and aching knees.

Wrapping, Splinting, and Slinging an Injury

When wrapping an injury, begin at the farthest point from the heart. Wrap the injury gently. You should wrap from slightly below the injury to slightly above it. Splinting an injury helps keep it still. To make a splint, you will need something that can be made stiff. Some examples are a rolled-up newspaper or a ruler. To secure the splint, you can use anything like a roll of gauze, rope, a belt, or tape. Slings elevate injuries of the arm and help prevent them from moving. To make your own arm sling, cut or fold a piece of cloth into a triangle. Place one end of the triangle over the shoulder of the uninjured arm. Fold the injured arm across your chest, making sure your fingers are higher than your elbow. Bring the other end of the triangle up and onto the shoulder of the injured arm. Tie the two ends of the triangle at the back of your neck. The third point of the triangle can be wrapped around your elbow and secured with a safety pin.

Chapter four

HOW SHOULD I DEAL WITH INJURY TO THE EYES, EARS, NOSE, AND MOUTH?

The three common causes of eye injury are a chemical splashed into the eye, a foreign object in the eye, and a blow to the eye. Chemicals, such as cleaning agents, can cause serious or permanent injury to the eye. They could even cause blindness. It is important that immediate action be taken to remove the chemical from the eye. (Chemicals, both on the skin and in the eye, continue to burn until they are removed.) To flush the chemical from the eye, hold the eyelid open and gently run cold water from a faucet on it for at least ten minutes. It is important to hold the head so that the injured eye is lower than the other eye. Otherwise, the chemical may flow into the healthy eye during rinsing. Once the chemical has been washed from the eye, cover the eye with gauze and seek immediate medical attention.

You should never attempt to remove an object that is sticking into the eyeball. You must seek immediate medical attention. In the meantime, gently cover both eyes. Both eyes need to be covered because when one eye moves, the other one moves as well. This movement could cause further damage to the injured eye. If the object embedded in the eye is large, tape a cup over the eye. This will keep the object from getting pushed farther in.

Particles like eyelashes, dirt, or sand that are floating on the eyeball or inside the eyelid may be carefully removed. First, wash your hands with soap and water. Then gently pull the top eyelid down over the lower eyelid. This will cause tears to flow and may wash out the particle. If this doesn't work, rinse the eye by gently running warm water over it. If the particle is still there, you can use a moist cotton swab or the corner of a soft cloth to lightly touch the object. It should come right out. If the eye remains teary, painful, or scratchy, you should see a doctor. There may be a scratch on the cornea (the clear covering on the front of the eye). There may also be something stuck in your eye that is too small for you to see.

A black eye is a common result of a blow to the eye area or the forehead. The area around the eye will get puffy. It often turns black and blue. This discoloration is caused by blood leaking into the tissues around the eye like a bruise. A black eye should be iced immediately for at least ten minutes. This will reduce the amount of swelling and bruising. The bruising around the eye should go away in about two to three weeks. Though the injury may not look serious, there may be internal

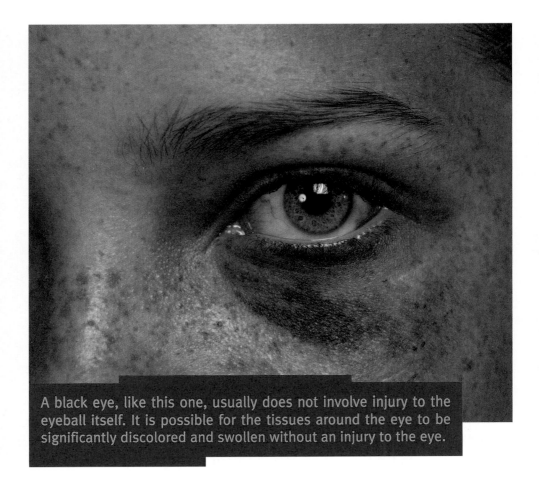

A black eye, like this one, usually does not involve injury to the eyeball itself. It is possible for the tissues around the eye to be significantly discolored and swollen without an injury to the eye.

bleeding in the eye or injury to the bone surrounding the eye. See a doctor if there is any bleeding in the white or colored part of the eye or if you experience blurred or double vision. Anytime there is a head injury, you should seek immediate medical attention if there is bleeding from the mouth or nose, a change in pulse, severe headache, difficulty breathing, severe vomiting, slurred speech, unequal eye pupils, or unconsciousness.

Ear Injury

There are many reasons that an ear can hurt. Two common causes are middle ear infections and external ear infections—for example, swimmer's ear, which can be caused by swimming in contaminated water. Both middle ear and external ear infections require medical attention. If blood or clear fluid is ever flowing out of the ear, seek medical attention right away. This may indicate a serious head injury. Bleeding from the ear may also be the result of a ruptured eardrum. A ruptured eardrum can be caused by loud noise, infection, diving into deep water, or head injury. In addition to bleeding from the ear, a ruptured eardrum also brings about hearing loss. With any bleeding from the ear, do not put anything in the ear to absorb the blood. Turn the head so that the blood can drain out (unless you suspect neck injury), loosely cover the ear with a clean cloth, and get medical help immediately.

Sometimes an insect may fly into an ear and become stuck. If the insect is alive and buzzing, you can put several drops of warm (body temperature) oil into the ear. This will suffocate the bug and it should float out. If the insect does not come out, see a doctor to remove it. Small objects, such as beads, beans, paper, and pebbles, can become stuck in the ear. In this case, do not put water or oil in the ear to flush the small object out. This could cause some objects to swell and become much more difficult to extract. Objects that are stuck in the ear require medical attention for removal. However, if paper or cotton is stuck in the ear and is clearly visible, you may remove it carefully with a pair of tweezers.

This man is properly controlling a nosebleed by leaning forward and pinching his nose shut.

Nose Injury

Nosebleeds may look bad, but usually they are not very serious. Many of the blood vessels in the nose are located close to the surface of the nasal lining and are easily injured. Nosebleeds may be caused by any kind of damage to the nose, such as scratching the nasal lining, blowing the nose too hard, or bumping the nose. They also may be caused by dryness of the nasal lining.

In most cases, nosebleeds are very easily controlled. If you get a nosebleed, sit down and lean slightly forward. Pinch your nose shut for at least ten minutes, keeping your mouth open so that the blood or blood clots will not block your airway. A cold washcloth applied to the nose and the surrounding area may help constrict the blood vessels and thus stop the bleeding. After the nosebleed stops, don't blow your nose for several hours.

If the bleeding has not stopped after thirty minutes, seek medical treatment. You should also see a doctor if you suspect that your nose is broken. Seek immediate medical attention if a nosebleed or a leakage of clear fluid starts after a head injury. This could indicate a fracture at the base of the skull. You can prevent nosebleeds by blowing your nose gently, not picking your nose, and using a humidifier to moisten the lining of the nose in hot climates or in the winter when the heat is on indoors. Drinking plenty of water also helps keep your body hydrated.

If an object gets lodged in your nose, don't try to expel it by breathing forcefully through your nose. Instead, breathe through your mouth until the object has been removed. You may try to blow your nose gently to see if that will dislodge the object. However, don't blow hard or repeatedly. If the object is visible and can be easily reached with tweezers, you may try to remove it. Do not attempt to remove the object if it's not easily grasped with the tweezers because this could force it farther into the nostril. If you are unable to dislodge the object, seek medical assistance.

Mouth Injury

An injury may cause teeth to be chipped, broken, loosened, or even knocked out. If a tooth is chipped or broken, you can clean dirt from the area with warm water. Place a cold compress on the face near the area of the injured tooth to relieve pain and swelling. Go to the dentist at once and bring the broken or chipped piece of the tooth with you.

If a tooth is loosened or knocked partially out of its socket, press the tooth back into place and call your dentist. If your tooth has been completely knocked out, apply direct pressure to the empty socket to control bleeding. A dentist can often put the tooth back in its place, so make sure to save the tooth. When handling the tooth, avoid touching the roots. If the tooth is dirty, rinse it with milk but don't scrape, scrub, or dry it. You can transport the tooth to the dentist in a container of milk, which is a good preservative because its chemical makeup is compatible with teeth. Never place an aspirin next to an aching tooth. This can cause a chemical burn on the cheek or gums.

Protective gear should be worn while playing sports in order to prevent injury. This boy is wearing a helmet to protect his head and a mouth guard to protect his teeth.

Common products can cause injury to the soft tissue of the mouth. For example, if you use mouthwash several times a day, the mouthwash could kill the harmless bacteria in your mouth. This could cause a growth of harmful bacteria and result in infection. You should stop using any product that irritates the inside of your mouth.

If the tongue or lips are bitten deeply or cut, they will bleed excessively. To control the bleeding, apply a constant, direct pressure for at least five minutes (without checking in between to see if the bleeding has stopped). Place a piece of gauze between the thumb and forefinger to help grip the tongue. Squeeze the edges of the cut together. If there is swelling or pain, a cold compress can be used. If you can't get the bleeding to stop, seek immediate medical attention.

To prevent injuries to the mouth, wear the proper safety gear when playing sports. Don't bite or chew on objects like pencils, and don't use your teeth to open things. You should also avoid biting down on hard items, such as ice, popcorn kernels, or nutshells.

Myths and Facts

Applying a raw steak to a black eye will help it heal faster.

Fact: ➻ Putting raw meat on your eye could contaminate the eye with bacteria, such as *E. coli*. Putting something cold on the eye is what is important. Crushed ice works best. Or try a bag of frozen peas.

You should never use tweezers to remove a bee stinger.

Fact: ➻ Though using tweezers to remove a bee stinger could force more venom into the skin, speed is what counts the most. How fast the stinger is removed is much more important than how it is removed. If you are unable to scrape it out with something like a credit card or your fingernail, you may go ahead and use tweezers.

You should use hydrogen peroxide to clean a cut.

Fact: ➡ Hydrogen peroxide can actually delay the healing of a cut. It not only kills bacteria, but it also kills the cells that your body has rushed to the wound to heal it. The best way to clean a scrape or cut is to wash it gently with soap and water.

Applying butter is good treatment for a burn.

Fact: ➡ Butter and other oils will actually cause burned skin to retain heat, potentially causing more harm. It is better to apply a cold-water compress and, if there is no blistering, a little aloe vera ointment.

Chapter five

HOW SHOULD I HANDLE SOME OTHER COMMON INJURIES?

Ailments of the digestive tract are rather common. For example, diarrhea is frequent, watery stools. Most times, diarrhea is not serious and does not last long. It can be caused by eating spoiled foods (food poisoning). It can be the result of allergies, mild viral infections, drinking alcohol, or emotional upset. For some people, milk or other dairy products can cause loose stools. Diarrhea may also be a side effect of some medications, especially antibiotics. Usually, diarrhea is accompanied by mild abdominal cramps and loss of appetite.

To treat diarrhea, avoid eating solid foods and drinking milk. Instead, try to consume only clear liquids like water, tea, ginger ale, and broth. Once the diarrhea has stopped, begin eating solid foods slowly. Start with bland foods like saltine crackers, rice, and dry toast.

Seek medical care if the diarrhea lasts longer than two days. Dehydration could occur. You should also seek medical attention right away if your stools are bloody or black in color. Also see a doctor if you have severe or prolonged stomach cramping.

Cold Weather Injuries

When your body is exposed to very low temperatures, it's in danger of freezing. When parts of the body freeze, ice crystals form in the tissue. This is called frostbite. The longer you are exposed to the cold, the greater the risk of damage. The parts of your body that are most likely to be frostbitten are the toes, fingertips, tip of the nose, and earlobes. These are particularly susceptible because they are far from the body's core heat.

In the early stages of frostbite, the skin appears red and is painful. However, as frostbite sets in, the pain disappears. The skin turns a white or grayish color and blisters may form. If you suspect that you have frostbite, you should get medical help immediately. Meanwhile, cover up the chilled part. You can cover it with extra clothing or a blanket. Putting frostbitten fingers in your armpits also works, as does covering frostbitten cheeks with bare hands. Do not rub the injured area. This will only cause the ice crystals in the tissue to do more damage. Try to get to a warm place, like in a house or a tent, if possible. You can then put the frostbitten area in warm water to thaw it. Do not use hot water, heating lamps, campfires, hot water bottles, or

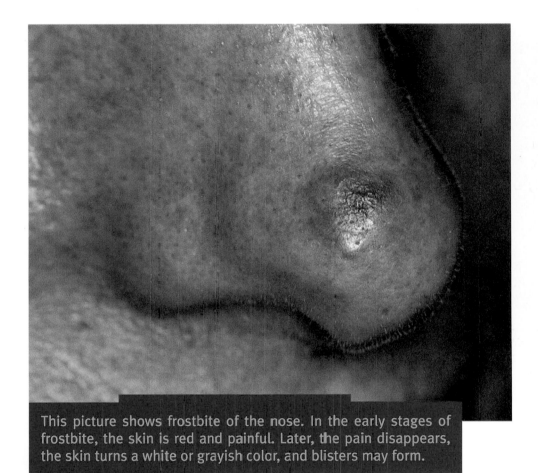

This picture shows frostbite of the nose. In the early stages of frostbite, the skin is red and painful. Later, the pain disappears, the skin turns a white or grayish color, and blisters may form.

heating pads on the injury. They are too hot. If you cannot get to a warm place and there is a chance that the part could refreeze, do not start the thawing process until you can get medical help.

Hypothermia is a chilling of the entire body. With hypothermia, body temperature drops so low that the body is unable to maintain its own heat. It's as if the body's furnace has gone out. For hypothermia to set in, conditions don't have to be extreme. It can be caused by any combination of cool weather, wet clothing, wind, hunger, or exhaustion. In fact, hypothermia often occurs when the temperature is well above freezing.

As the body cools, it begins to shiver in an attempt to create heat. Other symptoms of hypothermia include numbness, muscle weakness, and drowsiness. As the brain cools, the person may become disoriented and clumsy. In severe cases, a person's breathing could slow and the person could become unconscious. If you suspect that someone has hypothermia, seek medical help right away. Then begin warming the victim. Bring the person somewhere warm as quickly as possible. Remove all wet clothing and replace it with dry clothing and/or dry towels and blankets. Give the person warm liquids, such as soup or tea, to drink. The best way to help a person who is suffering from severe hypothermia in the wilderness is to remove his or her clothes and place the person between two other naked people. This allows heat to be transferred from the healthy people to the injured person.

To avoid frostbite and hypothermia, wear warm clothes when you are out in the cold. Putting on layers of clothes helps trap the heat. A water-resistant outer layer will keep wet clothes (which allow heat to escape) away from the body. Wearing a hat also helps you hold onto heat. Most of a person's heat is lost off the top of the head. You should also wear gloves. Before you go out in the cold, make sure that you've had plenty to drink. Eat to avoid dehydration and fatigue. Finally, do not ignore the signs that your body is under stress. For example, before frostbite begins, you would feel a "pins and needles" sensation.

Hot Weather Injury

Heat exhaustion occurs when the body becomes overheated and its attempts to cool itself down fail. It is often caused by someone doing strenuous physical activity in hot weather. The symptoms of heat exhaustion include pale and clammy skin, heavy sweating, headache, dizziness, nausea, fatigue, and heat cramps. Heat cramps are muscle spasms caused by a loss of salt and fluid from the body due to heavy sweating. To treat heat exhaustion, lie down in a shady place. Place a cool cloth on your forehead and drink plenty of cool water.

If heat exhaustion is not treated, it could lead to heat stroke. Heat stroke is a serious condition that could lead to death. With the onset of heat stroke, sweating lessens and the skin becomes hot, dry, and flushed. The body's temperature rapidly increases to temperatures of 102 degrees Fahrenheit (39 degrees Celsius) or higher. A person may feel disoriented or even faint. If this should happen, seek medical help immediately. In the meantime, the victim must be cooled down as quickly as possible. Remove the person's clothes and move him or her into the shade. Fan the person and place cold water or cold packs on the body. Dry the skin once the person's body temperature drops to about 101°F (38°C).

To prevent such injury, try to stay in the shade during hot weather. If you have to be out in the sun, wear a hat and light-colored clothing. You should avoid being in the sun for more than thirty minutes at a time. Plan to be out in the mornings or evenings. These are the coolest times of the day. Drink plenty of

When you are out in hot weather, drinking plenty of water can help you avoid conditions such as heat exhaustion and heat stroke.

water and eat a little more salt than usual at meals to help your body retain water.

Hot and humid weather can cause heat rash. Heat rash occurs when the body's sweat ducts are blocked. With heat rash, tiny red pinpoints cover the affected area. This rash can be treated with powders and soothing lotions. Heat rashes usually disappear when the victim enters a cool environment. However, see a doctor if the rash does not go away. Heat rashes can be avoided by wearing light, dry, loose clothing when out in hot weather.

Skin Poisoning

The oily substance, or resin, that is in some plants—like poison ivy, poison sumac, and poison oak—can irritate your skin. Skin poisoning from such plants causes redness, swelling, blisters, itching, fever, and headache. These symptoms usually last for about ten to fourteen days. Typically, the rash shows up a half day to two days after exposure to the plant, and blisters appear after a couple of days. You can treat a mild rash with calamine lotion or another soothing skin lotion. To relieve the itching, you can apply an ice pack or a damp cloth to the itchy spots. Sometimes a bath with either baking soda or oatmeal poured into the water can help the itch. However, if the rash is severe or is located on the face or genitals, you should see a doctor. You must also seek immediate medical attention if part of the plant is chewed or swallowed.

To prevent getting skin poisoning from a plant, learn to recognize the poisonous ones. Poison ivy grows as a plant, bush, or

Both the poison ivy plant *(top)* and the poison oak plant *(bottom)* grow with three shiny leaflets. The species are related.

vine. Its leaf is made up of three shiny leaflets. Poison sumac grows as a bush or tree. Its leaf has rows of two leaflets that are opposite each other, plus it has a leaflet at the top. The leaflets of the poison sumac are pointed at both ends. Poison oak may grow as a bush or vine. Its leaf has three leaflets.

In addition to avoiding poisonous plants, you should also avoid touching animals whose fur may have come into contact with the plants' oil. The oil from the plants can be transferred from an animal's fur to your skin or from clothing to your skin. Therefore, it is also wise to remove any clothing that may have touched the plants.

If you think you may have accidentally touched a poisonous plant, wash your skin well with soap and water. Then use alcohol and a wipe to clean the area. You should also not burn poison ivy, poison sumac, or poison oak. The oils from these plants are released into the air when they are burned. The tiny droplets could land on your skin and inside your nose and throat when inhaled.

Ten Great Questions to Ask Your Doctor

1 How often do I need to get a tetanus shot?

2 Is it OK to put butter or grease on a burn?

3 How do I know if I have an infection?

4 How can I remove a bee's stinger from my skin?

5 How can I know if I have Lyme disease?

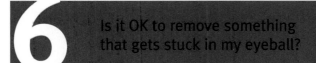

6 Is it OK to remove something that gets stuck in my eyeball?

7 How can I prevent getting skin poisoning?

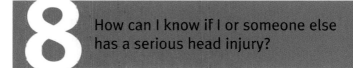

8 How can I know if I or someone else has a serious head injury?

9 How long will it take for my black eye to go away?

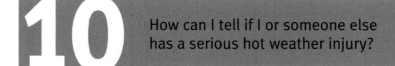

10 How can I tell if I or someone else has a serious hot weather injury?

abrasion Scraped area of the skin that has been damaged by rubbing or scratching.

alleviate To lessen pain.

antibiotic Substance that is able to kill bacteria.

antihistamine Drug used to treat allergies.

antiseptic Substance that kills bacteria and helps limit infection.

bacteria Microorganisms that cause illness.

blood vessel Any of the arteries, veins, or capillaries through which blood flows.

calamine lotion A pink lotion made from zinc oxide and ferric oxide that helps soothe irritated, itchy skin.

compression The act of applying pressure.

constrict To make narrower.

debris Fragments of something, such as broken-down pieces of rock.

disease A specific illness.

elevate To raise something up to a higher position.

fatigue Mental or physical exhaustion.

gauze Loosely woven cotton cloth used to dress wounds.

hypothermia Dangerous lowering of the body's core temperature.

laceration Torn, ragged wound.

ligaments Tough, elastic body tissues that connect bone and hold joints and organs in place.

mobility The ability to move.

nerves Fibers in the body that provide communication between the brain and the body.

ointment A smooth, greasy substance that is used on the skin.

pus A usually yellowish-white fluid found at the site of infection; it is made up of dead tissue, dead bacteria, and white blood cells.

sterile Free from bacteria or other microorganisms.

superficial Located at or near the surface.

swelling The enlargement of a part of the body with fluid accumulation, usually due to illness or injury.

tetanus Potentially fatal disease caused by bacterial infection.

tissue A grouping of similar cells in an organism.

venom A poisonous fluid that is injected by an animal, such as a snake.

virus A nonliving particle that consists of genetic material inside a protein capsule.

Information

Academy of Emergency Training
#125-4010 Regent Street
Burnaby, BC V5C 6N1
Canada
(604) 922-2249
Web site: http://www.firstaid.ca
   The Academy of Emergency Training is a school of
   instruction that is overseen by doctors, paramedics, and
   other health personnel.

American CPR Training
449 Santa Fe Drive, #127
Encinitas, CA 92024
(760) 944-1048
Web site: http://www.cpr-training-classes.com
   American CPR Training offers cardiopulmonary resuscitation
   (CPR), first aid, and other safety training in the United
   States, Canada, and Mexico.

American Red Cross
2025 E Street NW
Washington, DC 20006
(800) RED-CROSS (733-2767) or (800) 257-7575
Web site: http://www.redcross.org/index.html

The American Red Cross offers disaster relief, community services for the needy, support for military members and their families, the distribution of blood, and educational programs that promote health and safety.

BC First Aid
6010 Parkview Place
Sechelt, BC V0N 3A5
Canada
(877) 886-5867
Web site: http://www.bcfirstaid.ca
   BC First Aid provides CPR and first-aid instruction and related safety training.

Medic First Aid International
1450 Westec Drive
Eugene, OR 97402
(800) 800-7099
Web site: http://www.medicfirstaid.us
   Medic First Aid International is a worldwide leader in CPR/first-aid emergency care training programs for businesses, industries, and the public.

Nemours Foundation
10140 Centurion Parkway North
Jacksonville, FL 32256
(904) 697-4100
Web site: http://www.nemours.org

The Nemours Foundation is dedicated to improving the health of children.

Web Sites

Due to the changing nature of Internet links, Rosen Publishing has developed an online list of Web sites related to the subject of this book. This site is updated regularly. Please use this link to access the list:

http://www.rosenlinks.com/faq/evfa

Reading

American College of Emergency Physicians. *Pocket First Aid*. New York, NY: DK Publishing, Inc., 2003.

Boys Scouts of America. *Be Prepared First Aid*. New York, NY: DK Publishing, Inc., 2008.

Carney, John T. *Survival First Aid*. Broomall, PA: Mason Crest Publishers, 2002.

First Aid and CPR (Quamut Series). New York, NY: Barnes & Noble, 2007.

Thygerson, Alton L., and Benjamin Gulli. *First Aid*. Sudbury, MA: Jones and Bartlett Publishers, Inc., 2006.

Weber, Rebecca. *First Aid for You*. Mankato, MN: Coughlan Publishing, 2004.

index

A

allergic reactions, 20, 21, 45
animal bites, 14–17
antihistamines, 21

B

bee stings, 18–20, 43
black eyes, 35–36, 43
black widow spiders, 21–22
blisters, 8–10, 12, 13
brown recluse spiders, 21–22
burns, 10–13, 44
butterfly bandage, 6

C

calamine, 19, 24
cat bites, 14
cat scratch fever, 14
chiggers, 23–24
coral snakes, 17

D

diarrhea, 45–46
dislocation, 25–26
dog bites, 14
doughnut bandage, 10

E

ear injuries, 37
eye injuries, 34–36

F

fire ants, 20, 21
first-degree/superficial burns,
    11, 12
fleas, 23–24
fractures, 31–33, 39
frostbite, 46–48

G

gnats, 23–24

H

heat exhaustion, 49
heat rash, 51
heat stroke, 49
human bites, 14, 15, 17
hydrogen peroxide, 44
hypothermia, 47–48

I

incisions, 4–6
infection, signs of, 6, 8, 17

J

joints, 25–26, 28

L

lacerations, 4–6
lactic acid, 26

About the Author

Heather Hasan graduated from college summa cum laude, with dual majors in chemistry and biochemistry. She has written many books on the subjects of chemistry, biology, and health care. She currently lives in Pennsylvania with her husband, Omar, their sons, Samuel and Matthew, their daughter, Sarah, and their dog, Mofrey.

Photo Credits

Cover © www.istockphoto.com/Ron Sumners; p. 5 © Yoav Levy/ Phototake; p. 7 © Custom Medical Stock Photo; p. 9 © www.istockphoto.com/Nicole K. Cloe; p. 11 © www.istockphoto. com/Tammy Bryngelson; pp. 15, 38 © Dorling Kindersley; p. 16 © Raymond Gehman/Corbis; p. 19 © Educational Pictures/ Custom Medical Stock Photo; p. 22 © www.istockphoto.com/ William Howe; p. 27 © www.istockphoto.com/Jennifer Trenchard; p. 29 Phanie/Photo Researchers; p. 30 © www. istockphoto.com/Dana Bartekoske; p. 32 © www.istockphoto.com/ Nicholas Betton; p. 36 © www.istockphoto.com/Justin Horrocks; p. 41 © www.istockphoto.com; p. 47 © ISM/PhototakeUSA.com; p. 50 © Tom Pannell/Corbis; p. 52 (top) © www.istockphoto.com/ Chris Hill; p. 52 (bottom) © www.istockphoto.com/Nancy Nehring.

Designer: Nicole Russo; Editor: Christopher Roberts;
Photo Researcher: Marty Levick